CW00616585

Words of Comfort

Copyright © 1976 Lion Publishing

Published by
Lion Publishing plc
Sandy Lane West, Oxford, England
ISBN 0 7459 1969 3 (paperback)
ISBN 0 7459 2103 5 (cased)
Albatross Books Pty Ltd
PO Box 320, Sutherland, NSW 2232, Australia
ISBN 0 7324 0255 7 (paperback)
ISBN 0 7324 0460 6 (cased)

First edition in this format 1991
Photographs by Patricia and Charles Aithie - ffotograff.

Quotations from *Good News Bible*, copyright 1966, 1971 and 1976 American
Bible Society; published by the Bible Societies and Collins.

Printed and bound in Singapore

◆ *Words of* ◆
COMFORT

A LION BOOK

Oxford · Batavia · Sydney

◆ COME TO ME ◆

Come to me, all of you who are tired from carrying your heavy loads, and I will give you rest. Take my yoke and put it on you, and learn from me, for I am gentle and humble in spirit; and you will find rest. The yoke I will give you is easy, and the load I will put on you is light.

MATTHEW 11:28–30

◆ TRUST IN GOD ◆

But I will bless the person
    who puts his trust in me.
He is like a tree growing near a stream
    and sending out roots to the water.
It is not afraid when hot weather comes,
    because its leaves stay green;
it has no worries when there is no rain;
    it keeps on bearing fruit.

JEREMIAH 17:7–8

✦ THE PEACE OF GOD ✦

Don't worry about anything, but in all your prayers ask God for what you need, always asking him with a thankful heart. And God's peace, which is far beyond human understanding, will keep your hearts and minds safe, in Christ Jesus.

PHILIPPIANS 4:6–7

✦ THE SOURCE OF ALL ✦
BLESSING

The Lord says,
'I will bring my people back to me.
I will love them with all my heart;
     no longer am I angry with them.
I will be to the people of Israel like rain in a dry land.
They will blossom like flowers;
     they will be firmly rooted
     like the trees of Lebanon...

I will answer their prayers and take care of them;
Like an evergreen tree I will shelter them;
     I am the source of all their blessings.'

HOSEA 14:4–5, 8

◆ HELP IN TROUBLE ◆

Let us give thanks to the God and Father of our
Lord Jesus Christ, the merciful Father, the God
from whom all help comes! He helps us in all our
troubles, so that we are able to help those who
have all kinds of troubles, using the same help that
we ourselves have received from God. Just as we
have a share in Christ's many sufferings, so also
through Christ we share in his great help.

2 CORINTHIANS 1:3–5

◆ STRENGTH RENEWED ◆

Israel, why then do you complain
    that the Lord doesn't know your troubles
    or care if you suffer injustice?
Don't you know? Haven't you heard?
The Lord is the everlasting God;
    he created all the world.
He never grows tired or weary.
    No one understands his thoughts.
He strengthens those who are weak and tired.
Even those who are young grow weak;
    young men can fall exhausted.
But those who trust in the Lord for help
    will find their strength renewed.
They will rise on wings like eagles;
    they will run and not get weary;
    they will walk and not grow weak.

ISAIAH 40:27–31

◆ ALL WE NEED ◆

I prayed to the Lord and he answered me;
    he freed me from all my fears.
The oppressed look to him and are glad;
    they will never be disappointed.
The helpless call to him, and he answers;
    he saves them from all their troubles.
His angel guards those who fear the Lord
    and rescues them from danger.

Find out for yourself how good the Lord is!
    Happy is the man who finds safety in him!
Fear the Lord, all his people;
    those who fear him have all they need...

The good man suffers many troubles,
    but the Lord saves him from them all.

PSALM 34:4–9, 19

◆ YOU ARE MINE ◆

Israel, the Lord who created you says,
  'Do not be afraid—I will save you.
I have called you by name—you are mine.
When you pass through deep waters,
  I will be with you;
  your troubles will not overwhelm you.
When you pass through fire, you will not be burnt;
  the hard trials that come will not hurt you.
For I am the Lord your God,
  the holy God of Israel, who saves you.

ISAIAH 43:1–3

◆ GREAT COMPASSION ◆

'I turned away angry for only a moment,
    but I will show you my love for ever.'
So says the Lord who saves you.
'In the time of Noah I promised
    never again to flood the earth.
Now I promise not to be angry with you again;
    I will not reprimand or punish you.
The mountains and hills may crumble,
    but my love for you will never end;
    I will keep for ever my promise of peace.'
So says the Lord who loves you.

ISAIAH 54:8–10

◆ GOOD NEWS ◆

Jesus went to Nazareth, where he had been brought up, and on the Sabbath day he went as usual to the synagogue. He stood up to read the Scriptures, and was handed the book of the prophet Isaiah. He unrolled the scroll and found the place where it is written:

'The Spirit of the Lord is upon me.
He has anointed me to preach the Good News to the
    poor,
He has sent me to proclaim liberty to the captives,
    And recovery of sight to the blind,
To set free the oppressed,
    To announce the year when the Lord will save his
    people!'

Jesus rolled up the scroll, gave it back to the attendant, and sat down. All the people in the synagogue had their eyes fixed on him. He began speaking to them: 'This passage of scripture has come true today.'

LUKE 4:16–21

◆ GOD'S FLOCK ◆

Jerusalem, go up on a high mountain
    and proclaim the good news!
Call out with a loud voice, Zion;
    announce the good news!
Speak out and do not be afraid.
Tell the towns of Judah
    that their God is coming!
The Sovereign Lord is coming to rule with power,
    bringing with him the people he has rescued.
He will take care of his flock like a shepherd;
    he will gather the lambs together
    and carry them in his arms;
    he will gently lead their mothers.

ISAIAH 40:9–11

◆ THE GOOD SHEPHERD ◆

'I am the good shepherd. The good shepherd is willing
to die for the sheep. The hired man, who is not a
shepherd and does not own the sheep, leaves them
and runs away when he sees a wolf coming; so the wolf
snatches the sheep and scatters them. The hired man
runs away because he is only a hired man and does not
care for the sheep. I am the good shepherd. As the
Father knows me and I know the Father, in the same
way I know my sheep and they know me. And I am
willing to die for them.'

JOHN 10:11–15

◆ A PLACE PREPARED ◆
FOR YOU

'Do not be worried and upset,' Jesus told them. 'Believe in God, and believe also in me. There are many rooms in my Father's house, and I am going to prepare a place for you. I would not tell you this if it were not so. And after I go and prepare a place for you, I will come back and take you to myself, so that you will be where I am. You know how to get to the place where I am going.' Thomas said to him: 'Lord, we do not know where you are going; how can we know the way to get there?' Jesus answered him: 'I am the way, I am the truth, I am the life; no one goes to the Father except by me.'

JOHN 14:1–6

◆ SING PRAISE! ◆

The Lord is a refuge for the oppressed,
  a place of safety in times of trouble.
Those who know you, Lord, will trust you;
  you do not abandon anyone who comes to you.

Sing praise to the Lord who rules in Zion!
    Tell every nation what he has done!
God remembers those who suffer;
    he does not forget their cry.

PSALM 9:9–12

♦ GOD'S HAPPY PEOPLE ♦

Happy are those who know they are spiritually poor:
    the Kingdom of heaven belongs to them!
Happy are those who mourn:
    God will comfort them!
Happy are the meek:
    they will receive what God has promised!
Happy are those whose greatest desire is to do what
    God requires:
    God will satisfy them fully!
Happy are those who show mercy to others:
    God will show mercy to them!
Happy are the pure in heart:
    they will see God!
Happy are those who work for peace among men:
    God will call them his sons!

MATTHEW 5:3–9

◆ ETERNAL GLORY ◆

We know that God, who raised the Lord Jesus to life, will also raise us up with Jesus and take us, together with you, into his presence...

For this reason we never become discouraged. Even though our physical being is gradually decaying, yet our spiritual being is renewed day after day. And this small and temporary trouble we suffer will bring us a tremendous and eternal glory, much greater than the trouble. For we fix our attention, not on things that are seen, but on things that are unseen. What can be seen lasts only for a time, but what cannot be seen lasts for ever.

2 CORINTHIANS 4:14, 16–18

✦ ALL THINGS MADE NEW ✦

Then I saw a new heaven and a new earth. The first heaven and the first earth disappeared, and the sea vanished. And I saw the Holy City, the new Jerusalem, coming down out of heaven from God, prepared and ready, like a bride dressed to meet her husband. I heard a loud voice speaking from the throne: 'Now God's home is with men! He will live with them, and they shall be his people. God himself will be with them, and he will be their God. He will wipe away all tears from their eyes. There will be no more death, no more grief, crying or pain. The old things have disappeared.'

REVELATION 21:1–4